Let Us Pray

A Prayer Book

First published 2004 by
Veritas Publications
7/8 Lower Abbey Street
Dublin 1
Email publications@veritas.ie
Website www.veritas.ie

ISBN 1 85390 815 0

Designed by Colette Dower
Illustrations by Jeanette Dunne
Origination by Digital Prepress Imaging
Printed in the Republic of Ireland by Betaprint Ltd, Dublin

The Sign of the Cross

In the name of the Father,
And of the Son,
And of the Holy Spirit. Amen.

Comhartha na Croise

In ainm an Athar,
Agus an Mhic,
Agus an Spioraid Naoimh. Áiméan.

Glory be to the Father

Glory be to the Father,
And to the Son,
And to the Holy Spirit;
As it was in the beginning,
Is now and ever shall be,
World without end. Amen.

Glóir don Athair

Glóir don Athair,
Agus don Mhac,
Agus don Spiorad Naomh.
Mar a bhí ó thus,
Mar atá anois,
Mar a bheas go brách,
Le saol na saol. Áiméan.

God With Us

The arm of God be about us.
The light of Christ guide us.
The strength of the Holy Spirit support us.
Amen.

GOD THE FATHER

Our Father

Our Father who art in heaven
Hallowed be thy name.
Thy kingdom come,
Thy will be done on earth as it is in heaven.
Give us this day our daily bread
And forgive us our trespasses
As we forgive those who trespass against us.
And lead us not into temptation
But deliver us from evil. Amen.

An Phaidir

Ár nAthair atá ar neamh,
Go naofar d'ainm,
Go dtaga do ríocht,
Go ndéantar do thoil ar an talamh
Mar a dhéantar ar neamh.
Ár n-arán laethúil tabhair dúinn inniu,
Agus maith dúinn ár bhfiacha,
Mar a mhaithimidne dár bhféichiúna féin,
Agus ná lig sinn i gcathú,
Ach saor sinn ó olc. Áiméan.

GOD THE SON

Prayer to Jesus

Christ be with me.
Christ be beside me.
Christ be before me.
Christ be behind me.
Christ at my right hand.
Christ at my left hand.
Christ be with me
everywhere I go.
Christ be my friend
for ever and ever. Amen.

Paidir d'Íosa

Críost liom.
Críost romham.
Críost i mo dhiaidh.
Críost ionam.
Críost ar mo dheis.
Críost ar mo chlé.
Críost i mo chuideachta
is cuma cá dtéim.
Críost mar chara agam,
anois is go buan. Áiméan.

Care for me, Lord

Care for me, Lord,
As though you were a shepherd,
And I, a sheep of your flock.
Lead me to the comfort
Of quiet and peace.
Lead me to walk through the world
In your footsteps.
Even when there is sadness and shadow
I shall not be afraid
Or lose hope.
You are with me
In good times and in bad.
Care for me always, Lord,
As though you were a shepherd,
And I, a sheep of your flock.

Christy Kenneally

Tabhair aire dom, a Thiarna

Tabhair aire dom, a Thiarna,
mar a dhéanfadh aoire
agus mise mar chaora i do thréad.
Treoraigh mé go compord
an tsuaimhnis agus na síochána.
Treoraigh mé ionas go leanfaidh mé
lorg do choise tríd an saol.
Fiú nuair atá cumha agus scáth ann
ní bheidh eagla orm
ná ní chaillfidh mé dóchas.
Tá tusa liom
ag an dea-uair agus ag an drochuair.
Tabhair aire dom de shíor, a Thiarna,
mar a dhéanfadh aoire
agus mise mar chaora i do thréad.

GOD THE HOLY SPIRIT

Prayers to the Holy Spirit

Holy Spirit, I want to do what is right.
Help me.
Holy Spirit, I want to live like Jesus.
Guide me.
Holy Spirit, I want to pray like Jesus.
Teach me.

Spirit of God in the heavens.
Spirit of God in the seas.
Spirit of God in the mountain-tops.
Spirit of God in me.
Spirit of God in the sunlight.
Spirit of God in the air.
Spirit of God all around me.
Spirit of God everywhere.
Holy Spirit, Spirit of God, help me. Amen.

Holy Spirit, bright as flame,
Help our minds to understand.
Holy Spirit, cheerful as flame,
Keep us smiling and playful.
Holy Spirit, moving like flame,
Give us the energy to be good and kind. Amen.

Holy Spirit, Spirit of God,
Light our lives, move our hearts,
Our hands and our feet
So that in all that we think and do and say,
We will bring the Spirit of God
To our world this day. Amen.

Come Holy Spirit, fill the hearts of your faithful.
Enkindle in us the fire of your love.
Send forth your Spirit, and we shall be created,
And you shall renew the face of the earth.

O God, who has taught the hearts of the faithful
by the light of the Holy Spirit,
Grant us in the same spirit to be truly wise,
And ever to rejoice in his consolation,
Through Jesus Christ, our Lord. Amen.

Paidreacha don Spiorad Naomh

A Spioraid Naoimh, ba mhaith liom an rud ceart a
dhéanamh. Cabhraigh liom.
A Spioraid Naoimh, ba mhaith liom maireachtáil mar
a mhair Íosa. Treoraigh mé.
A Spioraid Naoimh, ba mhaith liom guí mar a ghuigh
Íosa. Múin dom é. Áiméan.

Spiorad Dé sna spéartha.
Spiorad Dé sna farraigí.
Spiorad Dé ar na sléibhte.
Spiorad Dé ionam.
Spiorad Dé i solas na gréine.
Spiorad Dé san aer.
Spiorad Dé thart timpeall orainn.
Spiorad Dé i ngach áit.
A Spioraid Naoimh, Spiorad Dé, cabhraigh liom.
Áiméan.

Tar, a Spioraid Naoimh, líon croíthe na bhfíréan
Agus las iontu tine do ghrá.
Cuir amach uait do Spiorad agus cruthófar iad,
Agus déanfaidh tú aghaidh na talún a athnuachan.

A Dhia, a mhúin croíthe na bhfíréan
le solas an Spioraid Naoimh,
Deonaigh dúinn sa spiorad céanna a bheith críonna
go fíor,
Agus gairdeas a dhéanamh i gcónaí ina shólás,
Trí Íosa Criost, ár dTiarna. Áiméan.

13

FROM THE PSALMS

Psalm 23

As a shepherd cares for his sheep,
So God cares for me.
Just as a shepherd brings his sheep
To meadows of green grass
And to cool, clear waters,
So God brings joy to my soul.
He guides me to good things.

Even though some days seem gloomy,
I know you are there to protect me.
You give me all I need and more than I need.
Your blessings overflow.
Ah, your goodness and kindness follow me
Every day of my life!
My home is with you, O God, as long as I live.

Psalm 23 for children

From Psalm 104

God, you make springs pour into the ravines.
They flow between the mountains.
They water all the wild animals.
The wild donkeys come there to drink.
Wild birds make nests by the water.
They sing among the tree branches.
You water the mountains from above.
The earth is full of the things you made.
You make the grass for cattle
and vegetables for the use of people.
You make food grow from the earth.

All these things depend on you
to give them their food at the right time.
When you give it to them
they gather it up.
When you open your hand,
they are filled with good food.

When you breathe on them
they are created.
You make the land new again.

I will sing to the Lord all my life.
I will sing praises to my God as long as I live.
My whole being, praise the Lord.

Psalm 104:10-14, 27-28, 30, 33, 35 from
International Children's Bible, New Century Version

Psalm 95

God our Creator,
People everywhere on earth
and beyond the sea trust you.
You make the mountains by your strength.
You have great power.
You are praised from where the sun rises to where it
sets.
You take care of the land and water it.
You make it fertile.
The rivers of God are full of water.
Grain grows because you make it grow.
You soften the ground with rain
and then you bless it.
You give the year a good harvest.
Everything shouts and sings for joy.

Based on Psalm 95
*from **Children's Bible, Contemporary English Version***

From Psalm 148

Sun and moon,
and all you bright stars,
come and offer praise.
Let all things praise the name of the Lord!
Sea monsters and the deep sea,
fire and hail, snow and frost,
and every stormy wind,
come, praise the Lord!

All mountains and hills,
fruit trees and cedars,
every wild and tame animal,
all reptiles and birds,
come, praise the Lord!

Every man and every woman,
young people and old,
come, praise the Lord!

Psalm 148:3, 5, 8-12
*from **Children's Bible, Contemporary English Version***

Praise God

Angels of the Lord, bless the Lord.
Galaxies and stars, bless the Lord.
Earth and moon and sun, bless the Lord.
Rain and wind and storm, bless the Lord.

Time and time and time again, praise God, praise God!

Light and dark, bless the Lord.
Night and day, bless the Lord.
Fire and heat, bless the Lord.
Ice and cold, bless the Lord.

Time and time and time again, praise God, praise God!

Lightning and clouds, bless the Lord.
Mountains and hills, bless the Lord.
Rocks and soil, bless the Lord.
All that grows, bless the Lord.

Time and time and time again, praise God, praise God!

Creatures that graze, bless the Lord.
Birds that fly, bless the Lord.
Fish in the sea, bless the Lord.
People of the earth, bless the Lord.

Time and time and time again, praise God, praise God!
Based on Psalm 148

FROM THE GOSPELS

The Beatitudes

Blessed are the poor in spirit, for theirs is the kingdom of heaven.
Blessed are those who mourn, for they will be comforted.
Blessed are the meek, for they will inherit the earth.
Blessed are those who hunger and thirst for righteousness, for they will be filled.
Blessed are the merciful, for they will receive mercy.
Blessed are the pure in heart, for they will see God.
Blessed are the peacemakers, for they will be called children of God.
Blessed are those who are persecuted for righteousness' sake, for theirs is the kingdom of heaven.

Matthew 5:3-10
*from **New Revised Standard Version Bible***

Be Blessed!

Be dependent on God, and be blessed!
Be mindful of those who had died, and be blessed!
Be close to the earth, and be blessed!
Be just and fair, and be blessed!
Be compassionate, and be blessed!
Be genuine and true, and be blessed!
Be a peacemaker, and be blessed!
Be prepared to stand up for what is right, and be blessed!
God will bless you when people insult you, mistreat you and tell lies about you because of me.

Based on the Beatitudes

The Commandments of Jesus

One of the teachers of the Law asked Jesus, 'What is the most important commandment?'

Jesus answered, 'The most important one says: People of Israel, you have only one Lord and God. You must love God with all your heart, soul, mind, and strength. The second most important commandment says: Love others as much as you love yourself. No other commandment is more important than these.'

Mark 12:28-31
*from **Children's Bible, Contemporary English Version***

The Kingdom of God

What is God's kingdom like? What story can I use to explain it? It is like what happens when a mustard seed is planted in the ground. It is the smallest seed in all the world. But once it is planted, it grows larger than any garden plant. It even puts out branches that are big enough for birds to nest in its shade.

Mark 4:30-32
*from **Children's Bible, Contemporary English Version***

The Lost Sheep

If any of you has a hundred sheep, and one of them gets lost, what will you do? Won't you leave the ninety-nine in the field and go look for the lost sheep until you find it? And when you find it, you will be so glad that you will put it on your shoulder and carry it home. Then you will call in your friends and neighbours and say, 'Let's celebrate! I've found my lost sheep.'

Luke 15:4-6
from Children's Bible, Contemporary English Version

Jesus dies on the Cross

Two criminals were led out to be put to death with Jesus. When the soldiers came to the place called 'The Skull', they nailed Jesus to a cross. They also nailed the two criminals to crosses, one on each side of Jesus. Jesus said, 'Father, forgive these people! They don't know what they're doing.'

Around midday the sky turned dark and stayed that way until the middle of the afternoon. Jesus shouted, 'Father, I put myself in your hands.' Then he died.

Luke 23:32-35, 44, 46
from Children's Bible, Contemporary English Version

God calls us to live in freedom

The Ten Commandments

First:

I am the Lord thy God, thou shalt not have strange gods before me.

Second:

Thou shalt not take the name of the Lord, thy God, in vain.

Third:

Remember that thou keep holy the Sabbath day.

Fourth:

Honour thy father and thy mother.

Fifth:

Thou shalt not kill.

Sixth:

Thou shalt not commit adultery.

Seventh:

Thou shalt not steal.

Eighth:

Thou shalt not bear false witness against thy neighbour.

Ninth:

Thou shalt not covet thy neighbour's wife.

Tenth:

Thou shalt not covet thy neighbour's goods.

First:

Love the Lord your God alone, with all your heart.

Second:

Respect the Lord's name.

Third:

Keep the Lord's Day holy.

Fourth:

Honour your parents.

Fifth:

All life is in God's hands; do not destroy life.

Sixth:

Be faithful in marriage.

Seventh:

Do not steal.

Eighth:

Do not speak falsely of others.

Ninth:

Do not desire a person who already belongs with another.

Tenth:

Do not be greedy for things that already belong to others.

St Paul tells his friends about love...

Love is kind and patient,
never jealous, boastful, proud, or rude.
Love isn't selfish or quick tempered.
It doesn't keep a record of wrongs that others do.
Love rejoices in the truth, but not in evil.
Love is always supportive, loyal, hopeful and trusting.
Love never fails!

1 Corinthians 13:4-8
*from **Children's Bible, Contemporary English Version***

St Paul tells us how to live as the Body of Christ

A body is made up of many parts, and each of them has its own use. That's how it is with us. There are many of us, but we are each part of the body of Christ, as well as part of one another.

Love each other as brothers and sisters and honour others more than you do yourself. Take care of God's needy people.

Ask God to bless everyone who mistreats you. When others are happy, be happy with them, and when they are sad, be sad. Be friendly with everyone.

Romans 12:4-5, 10, 13, 14-16
from Children's Bible, Contemporary English Version

MARY

Hail Mary

Hail Mary, full of grace,
The Lord is with thee.
Blessed art thou among women
And blessed is the fruit of thy womb, Jesus.
Holy Mary, mother of God,
Pray for us sinners,
Now, and at the hour of our death. Amen.

Sé do Bheatha, a Mhuire

Sé do bheatha, a Mhuire,
Atá lán de ghrásta,
Tá an Tiarna leat.
Is beannaithe thú idir mhná,
Agus is beannaithe toradh do bhroinne, Íosa.
A Naomh Mhuire, a mháthair Dé,
Guigh orainn, na peacaigh,
Anois agus ar uair ár mbáis. Áiméan.

Prayer to Mary

Mary, mother of Jesus,
I want to live and love like you.
I want to love the Father,
I want to love like Jesus. Amen.

Mother of Jesus, blessed are you.
Mother of Jesus, my mother too.
Help me to live like Jesus
And help me to live like you. Amen.

Paidir do Mhuire

A Mhuire, a Mháthair Íosa,
Teastaíonn uaim maireachtáil agus grá a thabhairt
cosúil leatsa.
Teastaíonn uaim grá a thabhairt don Athair.
Teastaíonn uaim grá a thabhairt mar a dhéanann Íosa.

A Mháthair Íosa, is beannaithe thú.
A Mháthair Íosa, is tú mo mháthairse freisin.
Cabhraigh liom maireachtáil cosúil le hÍosa,
Agus cabhraigh liom maireachtáil cosúil leatsa.
Áiméan.

The Angelus

The angel of the Lord declared unto Mary...
And she conceived by the Holy Spirit.
> *Hail Mary...*

Behold the handmaid of the Lord...
Be it done unto me according to thy word.
> *Hail Mary...*

And the Word was made flesh...
And dwelt among us.
> *Hail Mary...*

Pray for us, O holy Mother of God...
That we may be made worthy of the promises of
Christ.

Lord,
fill our hearts with your love,
and as you revealed to us by an angel
the coming of your Son as man,
so lead us through his suffering and death
to the glory of his resurrection,
for he lives and reigns with you and the Holy Spirit,
one God, for ever and ever. Amen.

Fáilte an Aingil

Tháinig aingeal an Tiarna le scéala chun Muire,
Agus ghabh sí ón Spiorad Naomh.
   'S é do bheatha, a Mhuire…

Féach, mise banóglach an Tiarna,
Go ndéantar liom de réir d'fhocail.
   'S é do bheatha, a Mhuire…

Agus ghlac an Briathar
Colainn daonna,
Agus chónaigh sé inár measc.
   'S é do bheatha, a Mhuire…

Guigh orainn a Naomh-Mháthair Dé
Ionas go mb'fhiú sinn gealltanais Chríost.

A Thiarna,
Líon ár gcroíthe le do ghrá,
Agus faoi mar a nocht tú dúinn trí aingeal
Teacht do Mhic i gcolainn daonna,
Treoraigh sinn, dá bhrí sin, trína fhulaingt agus a bhás
Go glóire a aiséirí,
Mar is é a mhaireann agus a rialaíonn
in éineacht leatsa agus leis an Spiorad Naomh,
Aon Dia, trí shaol na saol. Áiméan.

Memorare

Remember,
O most gracious Virgin Mary,
That never was it known
That anyone, who fled to your protection,
Implored your help,
Or sought your intercession,
Was left unaided.
Inspired with this confidence, I fly to you,
O Virgin of Virgins, my Mother.
To you I come;
Before you I stand,
Sinful and sorrowful.
O Mother of the Word Incarnate,
Do not reject my petitions,
But graciously hear and answer them.
Amen.

The Magnificat

My soul magnifies the Lord,
and my spirit rejoices in God my Saviour,
for he has looked with favour on the lowliness of his
servant.
Surely, from now on all generations will call me
blessed;
for the Mighty One has done great things for me,
and holy is his name.
His mercy is for those who fear him
from generation to generation.
He has shown strength with his arm;
he has scattered the proud in the thoughts of their
hearts.
He has brought down the powerful from their
thrones, and lifted up the lowly;
he has filled the hungry with good things,
and sent the rich away empty.
He has helped his servant Israel,
in remembrance of his mercy,
according to the promise he made to our ancestors,
to Abraham and to his descendants forever.

Luke 1:46-55
from New Revised Standard Version Bible

The Magnificat

My soul glorifies the Lord,
My spirit rejoices in God, my Saviour.
He looks on his servant in her lowliness;
Henceforth all ages will call me blessed.

The Almighty works marvels for me.
Holy his name!
His mercy is from age to age,
On those who fear him.

He puts forth his arm in strength
And scatters the proud-hearted.
He casts the mighty from their thrones
And raises the lowly.

He fills the starving with good things,
Sends the rich away empty.

He protects Israel, his servant,
Remembering his mercy,
The mercy promised to our fathers,
To Abraham and his sons for ever.

From ***The Divine Office***

Hail, Holy Queen

Hail, holy Queen, mother of mercy;
Hail our life, our sweetness, and our hope!
To you we cry, poor banished children of Eve;
To you we send up our sighs, mourning and weeping
in this valley of tears.
Turn then, most gracious advocate,
Your eyes of mercy towards us;
And after this our exile,
Show to us the blessed fruit of your womb, Jesus.
O clement, O loving, O sweet Virgin Mary.
Pray for us, O holy Mother of God, that we may be
made worthy of the promises of Christ. Amen.

OTHER TIMES

Prayer to the Guardian Angel

Angel sent by God to guide me,
Be my light and walk beside me;
Be my guardian and protect me;
On the paths of life direct me.
Amen.

Paidir chuig an Aingeal Coimhdeachta

A Aingil dhil Dé, cuir mé faoi do smacht,
mar d'ordaigh Mac grámhar Dé ina reacht.
Seas le mo thaobh gach am den lá.
Soilsigh is cosain is seol mé slán.
Áiméan.

Morning Prayer

Father in heaven, you love me,
You're with me night and day.
I want to love you always
In all I do and say.
I'll try to please you, Father.
Bless me through the day. Amen.

Paidir na Maidine

A Dhia, tá grá agat dom.
Bíonn tú liom de lá is d'oíche.
Ba mhaith liom grá a thabhairt duit
Gach nóiméad den lá.
Ba mhaith liom tú a shásamh.
A Athair, cabhraigh liom. Áiméan.

Night Prayer

God, our Father, I come to say
Thank you for your love today.
Thank you for my family,
And all the friends you give to me.
Guard me in the dark of night,
And in the morning send your light. Amen.

Paidir na hOíche

A Dhia, a Athair, molaim thú
As ucht do chineáltais liom inniu.
As ucht mo chairde molaim thú,
Agus as an teaghlach a thug tú dom.
I ndorchadas na hoíche cosain mé;
Solas na maidine go bhfeice mé. Áiméan.

Journey Prayer

Arise with me in the morning.
Travel with me through each day.
Welcome me on my arrival.
God, be with me all the way. Amen.

Paidir Thurais

Éirigh liom, a Dhia,
Fan liom i rith an lae,
Sa bhaile agus ar gach turas,
Ná lig dom dul ar strae. Áiméan.

Grace before Meals

Bless us, O God, as we sit together.
Bless the food we eat today.
Bless the hands that made the food.
Bless us, O God. Amen.

Altú roimh Bhia

Beannacht ó Dhia orainne atá ag suí chun boird le
chéile.
Beannacht ar an mbia a ithimid inniu.
Beannacht ar na lámha a d'ullmhaigh dúinn é.
Beannacht, a Dhia dhílis, orainn féin. Áiméan.

Grace after Meals

Thank you, God, for the food we have eaten.
Thank you, God, for all our friends.
Thank you, God, for everything.
Thank you, God. Amen.

Altú tar éis Bhia

Go raibh maith agat, a Dhia, mar is tú a thug bia
dúinn.
Go raibh maith agat, a Dhia, mar is tú a thug cairde
dúinn.
Go raibh maith agat, a Dhia, mar is tú a thug gach
rud dúinn.
Go raibh maith agat, a Dhia. Áiméan.

Prayer before Playing

Praise God for the fun of it.
Glory to God for the friends in it.
Fair play to God for it.

Paidir roimh Imirt

Moladh le Dia as ucht an spóirt atá ann.
Glóir do Dhia as ucht na gcairde atá ann.
Fair play dhuit, a Dhia, as ucht an spraoi a bheith ann.

Prayer after Playing

Thank God for the fun of it.
Thank God for the friends in it.

Paidir i ndiaidh Imeartha

Buíochas le Dia as ucht an spóirt a bhí ann.
Buíochas le Dia as ucht na gcairde a bhí ann.

Prayer on opening the Bible

Bless me, O God, so that
in opening this Bible
I may open my mind and my heart
to your word.
May it nourish me
as it nourished Jesus. Amen.

Paidir ar an mBíobla a oscailt

Beannaigh mé, a Dhia, ionas
nuair a osclaím an Bíobla seo
go n-osclóidh mé m'intinn agus mo chroí
do do Bhriathar.
Go gcothaí sé mé
faoi mar a chothaigh sé Íosa.
Áiméan.

Prayer on closing the Bible

Bless me, O God,
so that in closing this Bible
I may enclose your word
in my heart and in my mind
as Jesus enclosed it in his.
Amen.

Paidir ar Bhíobla a dhúnadh

Beannaigh mé, a Dhia,
agus an Bíobla seo á dhúnadh agam
go gcoinneoidh mé do Bhriathar
i mo chroí agus i m'intinn
faoi mar a rinne Íosa.
Áiméan.

When someone has died...

Gentle God,
you love all of us.
Wipe away the tears of those who are sad
and help all of us to remember Jesus
who died and rose from the dead.
May we live for ever with Jesus
and be happy for ever. Amen.

FOR THE SACRAMENT OF RECONCILIATION (CONFESSION)

Act of Sorrow

O my God, I thank you for loving me.
I am sorry for all my sins,
for not loving others and not loving you.
Help me to live like Jesus and not to sin again. Amen.

An Gníomh Dóláis

A Dhia, gabhaim buíochas leat as ucht do ghrá dom.
Tá brón orm faoi mo pheacaí uile:
Nach raibh grá agam duitse ná do dhaoine eile.
Cabhraigh liom mo shaol a chaitheamh ar nós Íosa
Agus gan peaca a dhéanamh arís. Áiméan.

Prayer for Forgiveness

O my God, help me to remember the times
when I didn't live as Jesus asked me to.
Help me to be sorry and to try again. Amen.

Paidir ag iarraidh Maithiúnais

A Dhia, ár nAthair, cabhraigh liom cuimhneamh ar na
huaireanta nár mhair mé mar a d'iarr Íosa orm.
Cabhraigh liom brón a bheith orm
agus iarracht eile a dhéanamh. Áiméan.

Prayer after Forgiveness

O my God, thank you for forgiving me.
Help me to love others.
Help me to live as Jesus asked me to. Amen.

Paidir tar éis Maithiúnais

A Dhia, ár nAthair, go raibh maith agat faoi
mhaithiúnas a thabhairt dom.
Cabhraigh liom grá a thabhairt do dhaoine eile.
Cabhraigh liom maireachtáil mar a d'iarr Íosa orm.
Áiméan.

I'm Sorry God

Sometimes God I do not care,
I'm selfish and I do not share.
I'm sorry God,
Now I've come to know…

God wraps us in his love each day,
Speaks gently to us on our way.
Even when we disobey,
God's love is always there.
God loves us every day.

Sometimes God I tell a lie,
Or hurt my friends and make them cry.
I'm sorry God,
Now I've come to know…

God wraps us in his love each day,
Speaks gently to us on our way.
Even when we disobey,
God's love is always there.
God loves us every day.

When I'm angry God, I shout,
I scream, I stamp and I give out.
I'm sorry God,
Now I've come to know…

God wraps us in his love each day,
Speaks gently to us on our way.
Even when we disobey,
God's love is always there.
God loves us every day.
Mary Amond O'Brien

THE SAINTS

Advent Prayer to John the Baptist

In our work, John,
help us to be fair.
Of those less fortunate, John,
help us to take care.
With those who have less, John,
help us to share.
For the One who is coming, John,
help us to prepare.

Prayer of St Francis of Assisi

Lord, make me an instrument of your peace:
Where there is hatred, let me sow love;
Where there is injury, pardon;
Where there is despair, hope;
Where there is doubt, faith;
Where there is darkness, light;
And where there is sadness, joy.

O Divine Master, grant that I may not so much seek
To be consoled as to console;
To be understood as to understand;
To be loved as to love;
For it is in giving that we receive;
It is in pardoning that we are pardoned;
And it is in dying that we are born to eternal life.

Paidir Phroinsias Assisi

A Thiarna, déan díom cuisle do shíochána:
San áit a bhfuil fuath, go gcuire mé grá;
Áit a bhfuil éagóir, pardún;
Áit a bhfuil amhras, creideamh;
Áit a bhfuil éadóchas, dóchas;
Áit a bhfuil dorchadas, solas;
Agus áit a bhfuil brón, lúcháir.

A Mháistir Dhiaga, deonaigh gur mhó liom
Sólás a thabhairt ná a fháil;
Gur mhó liom go dtuigfinn ná go dtuigfí mé;
Go mba mhó liom grá a thabhairt ná a fháil.
Óir nuair a thugaimid uainn, tugtar dúinn;
Nuair a thugaimid maithiúnas, ansin is ea a mhaitear
dúinn;
Agus is ar éag dúinn a shaolaítear sa bheatha shíoraí
sinn.

Litany of St Brigid

St Brigid, woman of prayer, pray for us.
St Brigid, generous and kind, pray for us.
St Brigid, who fed the hungry, pray for us.
St Brigid, who welcomed everyone, pray for us.
St Brigid, who spoke about Jesus, pray for us.
St Brigid, who lived like Jesus, pray for us.
St Brigid, you still care for everyone, pray for us.
St Brigid, protect us all, pray for us.
St Brigid, raised up to heaven, pray for us.
St Brigid, Patron of Ireland, pray for us.

St Patrick's Prayer

I arise today
Through the strength of heaven;
Light of sun,
Radiance of moon,
Splendour of fire,
Speed of lightning,
Swiftness of wind,
Depth of sea,
Stability of earth,
Firmness of rock.

I surround myself today with the power of God:
God's strength to comfort me,
God's might to uphold me,
God's good sense to guide me,
God's eye to look before me,
God's word to speak for me,
God's hand to lead me,
God's way to lie before me,
God's angels to save me.

Paidir Phádraig

Éirím inniu
Trí neart na bhflaitheas;
Solas na gréine,
Loinnir na gealaí,
Spleodar na tine,
Luas na tintrí,
Gastacht na gaoithe,
Doimhneacht na farraige,
Seasmhacht an domhain,
Daingne na carraige.

Tá cumhacht Dé umam inniu:
Brí Dé dom chumhdach,
Neart Dé mar thaca agam,
Stuaim Dé dom threorú,
Súil Dé mar chonair romham,
Briathar Dé mar chomhairle agam,
Lámh Dé dom stiúradh,
Bóthar Dé os mo chomhair amach,
Aingil Dé do mo shábháil.